The Little Book
of Golf Slang

To Steve -
Next time you're in
the neighborhood let's
play some golf. I hope you
enjoy the book.

Randy Yorkess

The Little Book of Golf Slang

From Fried Eggs to Frog Hairs,
Words to Help You Pass as a Golfer

RANDY VOORHEES

A Mountain Lion Book

**Andrews McMeel
Publishing**

Kansas City

www.andrewsmcmeel.com

ISBN: 0-8362-3532-0

Library of Congress Catalog Card Number: 97-71630

ATTENTION: SCHOOLS AND BUSINESSES

Andrews McMeel books are available at quantity discounts with bulk purchase for educational, business, or sales promotional use. For information, please write to: Special Sales Department, Andrews McMeel Publishing, 4520 Main Street, Kansas City, Missouri 64111.

For Mom and Dad,
who taught me the right way.

And for Carol,
the love of my life.

Acknowledgments

I want to extend my thanks to John Monteleone, my boss, who encouraged me to write this book. To Matt Lombardi, my editor, many thanks for believing in this book. To my pal, Mike Corcoran (alias the Crusher), who facetiously refers to me as the Shot-maker—thanks, and may your next tee shot be a sniper bound for East Borneo. And to golfers every-where—both good and bad—thank you for your creative vocabularies.

A game The very best golf you can play. A phenomenon seldom experienced by normal golfers, the *A game* is what Greg Norman seems to bring to the golf course every day—except Sunday.

ace A hole in one. Like an *ace* in a deck of cards, though not quite so common.

afraid of the dark What a putt is when it won't go in the hole.

airmail To hit a shot much farther than planned (most commonly over the green). Amateur golfers frequently *airmail* approaches to greens fronted by hazards.

albatross Another name for a double eagle, a score of three under par on a hole. The most famous *albatross* in golf's history was recorded by Gene Sarazen on the fifteenth hole at Augusta National Golf Club during the 1935 Masters Tournament. A term generally not found in the amateur golfer's vocabulary.

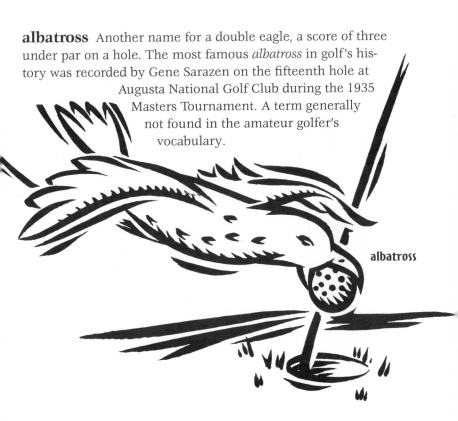

albatross

amateur side Derisive term for the low side of the hole when putting. Amateur golfers often miss their putts short, or come out on the low side of the hole, meaning the ball hasn't been struck boldy enough to have a chance of falling in. Although a missed putt counts one stroke no matter where it stops, balls that run by the hole are apparently more "professional."

army golf Phrase used to describe the inconsistent, wayward shots of amateur golfers, that is, "left-right, left-right" (like the drill sergeant's call during an *army* march).

Arnie's Army Name given to the legions of loyal fans who flock to tournaments to follow Arnold Palmer, golf's "king." Arnie has always been a fan favorite, and dozens of times his fans have kicked, blocked, or thrown a wayward Palmer shot back onto the fairway or green to help their hero.

back, the The final nine holes on a golf course.

backdoor The part of the cup located opposite the ball on the green. To reach the *backdoor,* a putt must curl around most of the hole before dropping in. Perhaps the most famous *backdoor* putt is the one sunk by Spain's Seve Ballesteros on the seventy-second hole of the 1984 British Open championship at St. Andrews to beat Tom Watson.

backhander A putt struck with the back of the putter blade. Sometimes golfers will do this in a casual fashion when the ball is very close to the hole. When they miss a *backhander*—and it happens often—amateurs often smile and record their score as though they had made the putt. This is known as *cheating*.

bag rat Caddie.

bail out What many golfers do to avoid trouble on the course. That is, they hit a shot in the direction opposite the trouble. If the trouble is on the right side, they *bail out* left. If the trouble is on the left side, they *bail out* right. This term can also be used to describe how a golfer (after calling in sick to work) exits his cart after seeing his boss approaching.

banana ball An especially curvaceous slice. A ball that starts to the right and continues to curve right until it nearly lands behind the golfer who hit it. This shot is one reason why the word *fore* is heard on the golf course nearly as often as more notorious four-letter words.

barky When one of your shots strikes a tree and you still make par for the hole, you have made a *barky*. Golfers often include a *barky* as one of their *junk* bets during a match.

be right An urgent request a golfer makes of his ball during its flight to the green, usually occurring when the ball appears to be on line with the flagstick and the only doubt is whether the *right* club was used. The phrase is also used frequently by caddies who want to keep their jobs.

be the ball Profound golfing advice uttered by Chevy Chase in the movie *Caddyshack*. Golfing geeks have picked up the expression and often use it during a round, to the great annoyance of their companions.

beach, the The bunkers and other sand-covered areas at a golf course are known collectively as *the beach*.

bite A ball is said to *bite* when it is hit with sufficient backspin to make it stop quickly—or even roll backward—on the green. *Biting* carries its own satisfaction, but remember, it only helps if it brings the ball *closer* to the hole.

blade To hit a ball off the edge of an iron, thereby creating a shot that takes off like a line drive in baseball. Most often the shot will end up beyond its intended target. This shot is also said to be hit *thin*, or to be *skulled*. *Blade* is also a thin putter (no more than a half-inch wide) with a straight face. Little Ben, the famous putter owned by Ben Crenshaw, is an example of a *blade* putter.

blood, no Phrase used most often in match-play situations to indicate that the hole was halved, or played even, and no money has been won or lost.

blow up To have your golf game come apart at the seams. Easily recognized: When your score is *blowing up,* so are you.

Bo Derek A perfect shot. The expression comes from Ms. Derek's role in the movie *10*, in which some considered her as attractive as a 350-yard drive down the middle of the fairway.

Bob Barker A shot that's hit too high to be effective, so called because we ask it to "come on down."

bogey train A series of consecutive bogies. For professional golfers, the *bogey train* is a one-way ride to a job at a driving range.

bogey train

bomb A very long shot, usually a drive. John Daly hits *bombs*. Tiger Woods hits *bombs*. Most amateurs are content to hit firecrackers.

borrow On a breaking putt, the amount of distance aimed to the right or left of the cup. The greens at August National (where the Masters Tournament is held each year) are so severely sloped that golfers may have to *borrow* fifteen or twenty feet when lining up their putts. *Borrow* too much or too little, and you'll wind up borrowing to pay your gambling debts.

boss of the moss A golfer who is especially proficient on the green. On the PGA Tour, Loren Roberts is commonly called *"the boss of the moss"* because of his putting prowess.

brassie A two wood. Or, the balls of an opponent who asks for a four-foot gimmee on a putt for par.

breakfast ball Another way of saying *mulligan*. Derived from the fact that many players eat breakfast just before teeing off and may require two tries to hit a good tee shot on the first hole.

broom A term used to describe the putting stroke, since the motion involved in using a *broom* is similar. Many amateurs, though, are far more proficient at sweeping the garage than getting down in two.

brother-in-law act Alternating excellent play by partners in a two-ball match. Getting *brother-in-lawed* means your opponents took turns beating your brains in.

broom

bunt A controlled shot struck more for accuracy than distance; usually follows a low trajectory and runs a long way after hitting the ground. Nick Faldo and Lee Trevino are two accomplished golfers who *bunt* the ball to avoid the wind or to make sure the ball finds the fairway. For fun, you can also use the term to describe a less-than-prolific drive hit by an opponent, for instance, "Nice *bunt*, ace."

burner A tee shot that's hit low and hard.

butterfly with sore feet, like a An expression used by the more poetic golfers to describe a shot that lands very softly on the green.

butterfly with sore feet

buttonhook A putt that hits the cup on one side and rolls all the way around the edge of the cup before coming out the front edge of the cup. Also called a *horseshoe*. Either way, very nasty.

cabbage Deep, thick, inescapable rough. Also called *spinach*. Green, leafy vegetables are not good for your golf game.

can The hole. The cup. The place to put your putts. When you sink a putt, you *canned* it.

carpet The green. Soft, well-manicured fairways are also referred to as being "like *carpet*."

cart girl The lovely young lady who operates the beer cart (a motorized vehicle that carries refreshments to golfers out on the course). These refreshments typically cost a fortune, which probably explains why golf courses hire beautiful young women to sell them.

cart golf Term for when two golfers riding in the same golf cart repeatedly hit the ball in the same direction (usually into the rough). An efficient but not necessarily pleasant way to play.

cellophane bridge An invisible cover over the top of the cup that keeps golf balls from falling in. (The expression was popularized by TV golf analyst Gary McCord.)

Center City A tee shot that lands directly in the *center* of the fairway has gone to *Center City*.

center cut A putt that goes directly into the *center* of the cup.

Central America putt When a putt needs just one more revolution to fall into the hole. Get it? One more revolution?

chew Exclamation used by golfers who want their ball to stop—now! (See also *bite, grow teeth, growl, juice.*)

chili dip An improperly executed chip shot in which the club hits the ground before hitting the ball, usually resulting in a shot that rolls just a few inches. This is one shot you have in common with Jack Nicklaus because everyone who has ever played golf has done it. You've just done it a little more frequently than Jack.

Colonel Bogey Just another name for the dreaded score of one over par.

comebacker A shot that backs up after hitting the green. Or, for a high-handicapper, a tee shot that hits one of the tee markers and ends up behind you.

cop The ranger on the public golf course—the guy whose job it is to make sure the flow of play is smooth and all golfers are observing the game's etiquette. He's never around when the fivesome in front of you is too slow, but always around to watch you hit a tee shot out of bounds or into a lake.

cow pasture pool One of the less endearing names for the game of golf. Senior PGA Tour pro Robert Landers has given some legitimacy to the term by practicing his game alongside the "meadow muffins" on his dairy farm. *Cow pasture* is also used to describe poorly maintained golf courses.

cuppy A lie that's buried in a hole or depression.

cut A controlled shot that moves from left to right. Most golfers shout *"Cut!"* to their ball after they see it heading well to the left of their target, not realizing that this is not an "on-demand" feature of a golf ball.

dance floor The green. Perhaps the term comes from the smooth surface and relative flatness of the green, or maybe it is meant to convey the joy that accompanies finally making it there. One of the most famous dances performed on the green is the "saber dance" done by Chi Chi Rodriguez to celebrate a birdie.

dawn patrol The golfers who are the first to play each day, so named because they start their march around the course at sunrise.

dead When your ball is in a position from which you have no chance of getting it onto the green with your next shot. These positions include squirrels' nests and car windshields. (See also *jail*.)

deuce A score of two for any hole. Too many of these on your scorecard means you're probably only counting your tee shots.

dew sweepers Golfers who habitually play first in the morning; members of the *dawn patrol*.

die it in the hole The action of putting the ball so that it falls into the cup as it is *dying*, or losing the last of its momentum. Such strokes run the risk of becoming *Central America putts*, left on the *amateur side* of the hole.

digger A golfer who takes a big divot with his iron shots. A *digger's* swing takes a very steep approach to the ball. The opposite is a *picker*, a golfer who sweeps the ball off the ground with a flatter swing path.

dog track Derogatory term for a golf course that is not well maintained.

double Chen   Hitting the ball twice on the same shot. The term derives from the 1985 U.S. Open when tournament leader T. C. Chen suffered a disastrous two-stroke penalty for hitting his ball twice while attempting a shot from greenside rough. Rattled by his mistake, Chen was caught and passed by eventual champion Andy North.

double dip   In a four-ball match, a *double dip* occurs when you and your partner both birdie the same hole. The *dipping* is done by your opponents—into their pockets!

double sandy   A score of par or better on a hole where two shots are played from bunkers, most often recorded on a par four or par five where one sand shot is played from a fairway bunker and one shot from a greenside bunker. Amateurs rarely record a *double sandy*, but if they do they can collect because it's usually included as a *junk* bet.

down and dirty   Playing the ball "as it lies." No rolling the ball over or sitting it up. The way the game is meant to be played; your score is meaningless unless you play it *down and dirty*.

down the road   When you fail to qualify for the next round of play in a tournament. Also called *on your way home*.

downtown   Where the ball goes when you absolutely launch one from the tee. Borrowed from the baseball term for where a home run ball goes.

draino   Exclamation that follows the sinking of a putt, particularly a long putt.

dribbler   A shot that travels only a few feet, usually without getting airborne.

drive for show and putt for dough "He who putts the best wins the most." This timeless golf cliché supports the contention of some PGA Tour critics who say the professional game amounts to little more than a weekly putting contest.

drop kick When the club strikes the ground and then bounces into the ball. (See also *chili dip, dub, Gogolak*).

drop kick

dropped cat, like a Description of a ball with plenty of backspin that hits the green and hardly bounces.

dub To mishit a shot badly, causing it to roll on the ground and come to a stop far short of its target. A *dubber* is the guy in the group ahead who takes fourteen shots to reach the green and still insists he's having fun. (See also *hacker* and *duffer*.)

duck hook A shot that *ducks* to the left as soon as it is hit. More hazardous than a slice because it carries topspin and tends to roll farther after reaching the ground. As Lee Trevino once said, "You can talk to a fade, but a *hook* won't listen."

duffer A lousy golfer. A more friendly term than *hacker*. Your boss is a *duffer*; your brother-in-law is a *hacker*.

egg The ball, but only within the context of putting. You can putt, broom, or roll the *egg*, but you don't want to chip, pitch, or hit it.

elephant burial ground Collective term for the huge mounds found on the greens of certain golf courses. Where good scores often go to die.

elephant's ass A poorly struck shot that is "high and stinky." Usually applied to a popped-up drive that is higher than it is long. An *elephant's ass* might also prompt a comment such as, "Except for distance and direction, that was a good shot."

Fall Classic Pro golfer's term for the annual PGA Tour Qualifying Tournament, also known as Q-School. Each year young phenoms, journeyman pros, and fading veterans attend the *Fall Classic* in an attempt to win a membership card that will allow them to compete on the prestigious and lucrative PGA Tour. Because of the all-or-nothing nature of the competition, the pressure is incredible, enough at times to reduce the participants to tears.

fan To miss the ball completely. The air moves, but nothing else does.

fat, hit it To hit the ground behind the ball first so that the shot has no spin and does not achieve the desired distance. Results often resemble an *elephant's ass.* (See also *lay the sod over it.*)

feather To hit a controlled shot with a full swing. By slowing down the club-head speed, the golfer hits a shot that travels less distance than a full club would normally allow, causing the ball to land softly like a *feather*. The shot is popular in match play because it can confuse an opponent into thinking that more club is needed to hit a certain shot.

fight To struggle with a particular golfing flaw. If all your poor shots are slices, you're said to be *fighting* a slice. If all your misses are hooks, you're said to be *fighting* a hook. If you miss all your short putts, you're said to be *fighting* a balky putter. If your rounds resemble boxing matches, take up tennis.

first-tee syndrome The fear of hitting the first tee shot of the day, a devastating malady known to overcome many amateur golfers. Also known as *first-tee jitters*.

flame-broiled
Description of a drive
that is hit hard and
far. (As in a *Whopper*,
just like at Burger
King.)

flame-broiled

flat bellies The
younger, thinner golfers on
the PGA Tour. Coined by golfing
legend Lee Trevino.

flier A shot that flies
farther than normal
because of the way
the ball is lying

on the ground. *Fliers* often occur when the ball is sitting in light rough, where the blades of grass are growing toward the intended target, or when the ball is lying in clover, or when the ball is lying in wet grass. All of these scenarios eliminate backspin from the ball, thereby allowing it to fly through the air with less resistance. The term can also be used to describe the lie of the ball, as in a *flier* lie.

flop shot A high, delicate shot that travels only a short distance and then rolls very little once it lands on the green. Essentially, it is *flopped* onto the green. Not to be confused with a *dropped cat*.

flub A terrible shot. Putt, chip, pitch, drive—it doesn't matter. If you hit it bad, you *flubbed* it, buddy.

fluffy Description for a lie where the ball is sitting on top of the grass leaving room for the club face to travel under the ball. This lie allows for little spin to be imparted onto the ball. Chips and pitches hit from *fluffy* lies are often left short as the club goes under the ball rather than making solid contact with it.

flying elbow When the right elbow (for a right-handed golfer) is far away from the body on the downswing, usually meaning that the club is approaching the ball on an out-to-in path, thus causing the ball to slice. It was thought that anyone with a *flying elbow* could not play good golf until Jack Nicklaus flapped his way to being the greatest golfer in the history of the game.

four-jack To take four putts on a hole. Only tolerable for those who can drive the green on a par five. When asked how he *four-jacked* a hole at the Masters, Seve Ballesteros replied, "I miss. I miss. I miss. I make." Well said.

fried egg A ball buried in the sand, with a ring around it created on impact. Too many *fried eggs* will make you lose your appetite for the game.

frog hairs The short grass at the edge of the green. Also known as the *collar* or the *fringe.*

front, the The first nine holes of any golf course.

Frosty Nickname for the score of eight on a hole. Synonymous with *snowman* because the figure eight resembles a snowman and *Frosty* is the most famous snowman of all.

fuzzy Description for the condition of greens that haven't been mowed recently. Putting on *fuzzy* greens is more like putting in the fairway—slow! Also a nickname for PGA Tour golfer *F*rank *U*rban *Z*oeller.

gas What putts left on the *amateur side* of the hole run out of.

get down A message from golfer to ball asking it to cease flying—now! Usually heard after a ball is hit too far or off line; almost always uttered with great agitation.

get up The opposite of *get down*, an exhortation used to urge a putt or shot to travel farther toward the hole. Also used by Golfer A to urge Golfer B to regain consciousness after Golfer A has hit Golfer B in the head with an errant iron shot.

gimme A conceded putt, shortened from the phrase *"Give it to me."* *Gimmes* are the center of many golfing controversies, especially among the ranks of amateurs who are always looking for an opponent to concede a putt, even if their ball is off the green. (See also *good, good* and *in the leather*.)

give, give An agreement between a golfer and his opponent to *give* each other their next putt. Usually the result of two amateurs with a shared fear of the short game. (See also *good, good*.)

go to school To learn about the speed and direction of a putt or chip by observing another putt or chip on the same or similar line is golf's version of *going to school*. Smart golfers also *go to school* on their own putts and chips and watch as they roll past the hole to get a look at any break that will effect the putt coming back.

goat farm A poorly maintained golf course. (See also *dog track*.)

God squad Nickname for the group of PGA Tour players who hold regular prayer meetings at professional golf tournaments.

goer A shot that *goes* much farther than normal for the club being used. A member of the *flier* family.

Gogolak This synonym for *drop kick* gets its name from Charlie and Pete *Gogolak*, two former NFL placekickers.

golf lawyer A player known for constantly citing the rules, usually to the detriment of your score. This character may sound versed on the rules of the game, but he's probably trying to take advantage of you. If you're playing with a *golf lawyer,* carry a copy of the Rules of Golf with you at all times.

golf widow The wife of an obsessive golfer. She doesn't know who Jack Nicklaus is, and she doesn't care. Her husband will remember Jack's birthday before he remembers hers.

good, good See *give, give.* When two golfers have putts that lie similar distances from the cup, one player will say, "Your putt is *good* if mine is *good.*" Used mostly by amateur players who fear short putts.

greenie One of the many *junk* bets in golf, in which players in a foursome compete to see who can hit his ball on the green and closest to the hole on a par three. The golfer also must score a par or better to win the *greenie.*

grinder Term used for a golfer who is all business. A player whose only mission is to achieve the best score possible. A hard worker. A serious player. Boring. Tom Kite.

grip it and rip it To forget about all those "swing thoughts" and take a healthy *rip* at the ball. This phrase became popular after the prodigious swinger John Daly and his Herculean drives won the 1991 PGA title at Crooked Stick. When asked about his style, Daly said, "I just *grip it and rip it.*"

grocery money Winnings from a golf bet that the winner pledges to spend on food and drink, or *groceries*, usually at the *nineteenth hole*.

grounder A golf shot that never leaves the *ground*. (See also *worm burner*.)

grow teeth A golfer's plea for the ball to stop quickly. (See also *bite, chew,*

grow teeth

sitter, whoa down.) Also, something Tiger Woods did *after* he broke fifty for nine holes.

growl Action, backspin, *juice*. When you want your ball to stop quickly, you have to put some *growl* on it.

hacker A terrible golfer. A person who *hacks* it around the golf course. (See also *dub* and *duffer*.)

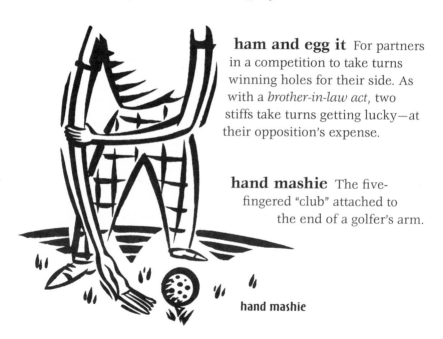

ham and egg it For partners in a competition to take turns winning holes for their side. As with a *brother-in-law act,* two stiffs take turns getting lucky—at their opposition's expense.

hand mashie The five-fingered "club" attached to the end of a golfer's arm.

hand mashie

hanging A lie where the ball is above the golfer's feet. Also what happens to a golfer caught using a *hand mashie*.

happy feet A nervous condition that afflicts golfers facing difficult shots. They just can't seem to get settled properly before taking their swing. A desirable trait to look for in potential betting opponents.

hit it in the head To hit the top of the ball. (See also *top*.)

hog's back A large mound used in the design of a golf green. (See also *elephant burial ground*.)

Hollywood Where you're at and what you are when everything is going just the way you want. Keep dreaming.

home hole The eighteenth and final hole on any golf course, so named because the golfer is approaching home— the *nineteenth hole.*

horses for courses Players (*horses*) who play certain courses well because those courses fit their style of play. Ben Hogan played Riviera Country Club very well, so the course became known as Hogan's Alley. Mark O'Meara plays Pebble Beach very well, having won there on four occasions. Whether you're a thoroughbred or a nag, you probably play some courses better than others.

hog's back

hooding the club A stroke in which the golfer moves his hands ahead and tilts the club head forward (to reduce the club's loft). Done to make the ball fly lower or to get more distance than normal from a club.

hot A ball that is traveling at a high rate of speed without much backspin (and many times at a lower trajectory than desired) is said to be *hot*. A ball may come into the green *hot* or out of the rough *hot*. In most cases, this shot will run along the ground or green much farther than desired, making the golfer *hot,* too.

hump When a caddie is carrying a golf bag around the course, he's *humping* it.

hunching Term for an illegal tactic in which a golfer inches closer to the hole when replacing a marked ball on the green. If your opponent hits his approach shot twenty feet from the hole but his first putt is only a fifteen-footer, add *huncher* to the list of names you call him.

hung it out A golfer who attempts to play a draw but hits a straight shot instead is said to have *hung it out*.

iffy lie A questionable lie, where it is uncertain how the ball will react when struck.

in The last nine holes of the course, also known as the *inward half*. You're moving *in* toward the clubhouse.

in his bag Expression used by a golfer who is confident in his ability to pull off a certain shot. The shot is *in his bag*.

in my pocket What a golfer tells the other members of his group when he's picked up his ball and conceded a hole. "I'm *in my pocket*." As a result, the other players are likely to be in his pocket, too—to take his cash.

in the hunt Term describing any player who has a chance of winning a tournament heading into its final stages. Alternatively, describes any *hacker* looking for his errant tee shot.

in the leather Phrase meaning a putt is close enough to the cup (a distance no greater than the length of the putter grip) to be conceded. (See also *gimme, give, give,* and *good, good*.)

in the linen Equivalent of *in my pocket*. Used by snappy dressers.

Is that any good? Rhetorical question posed to stunned opponents by a golfer who has just hit a career-best shot.

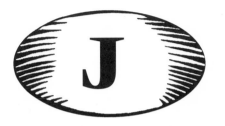

Jack and Jill event   A tournament played by one-man–one-woman teams.

jail   Where a golf ball usually lies after a *hacker* hits it. A place from which escape is nearly impossible. Deep rough, woods, buried lies, and other unpleasant places represent *jail* for a golf ball. (See also *dead*.)

jaws   The yawning chasm that is the front of the cup, when a putt stops inches short of its intended destination. For example, "He left it right in the *jaws*."

jelly legs   A disability that afflicts nervous golfers. (See also *happy feet*.)

jerk To pull a shot or putt left of the intended line. Also, a term used to describe a playing partner who pulls a shot or putt left of his intended line.

juice Backspin. (See also *growl*.)

juicy lie A lie in the rough where the ball is sitting atop the grass, offering a clean approach.

jump What a ball often does from a *flier* lie. That is, it *jumps* out *hot* and travels much farther than if struck from a normal lie.

jump on it To strike the ball with maximum force, with the hope of achieving maximum distance from the club used.

jungle The thickest, deepest, nastiest rough on the course.

junk Collective term for all golfing side bets. You can pick up *junk* from *barkies, greenies, nasties, sandies,* and, yes, even *birdies.*

jungle

keeper A successfully executed shot.

kick Literally, the way the ball bounces. Sometimes it *kicks* your way and sometimes it doesn't, but golfers are always asking for a *good kick*.

kill To hit the ball with great force. This was John Daly's "swing thought" during the 1991 PGA Championship at Crooked Stick. Before each shot his caddie, Jeff "Squeaky" Medlen, uttered one word: "*Kill*." Daly did.

knee-knocker A putt in the three-to-four-foot range that causes emotional and physical problems for the golfer. The term comes from the nervous trembling that accompanies these short putts. Every golfer experiences a *knee-knocker* at some time. (See also *throw-up range* and *yips*.)

knife The one iron. The toughest club to hit. If you carry a *knife* in your bag, you're either a real player or a phony who wants to look like a real player. A few swings with the *knife* will reveal the true you. Lee Trevino advises golfers caught in a lightning storm to hold their one irons aloft because "even God can't hit a one iron."

knockdown Term for a shot that is hit with an abbreviated follow-through to produce a low-trajectory, slight fade, and plenty of spin. A *knockdown* shot usually doesn't travel as far as a normal shot. This shot is employed when control is paramount. (See also *punch*.)

knockoff A club that is a clone or forgery of an original design. *Knockoff* clubs are attractive to golfers because they're so much less expensive than the clubs they imitate.

knuckleball A shot without spin that has an erratic flight. Some baseball pitchers find success with a *knuckleball*; golfers never do.

lag   To putt with the goal of getting the ball close to the hole rather than sinking it. Players *lag* putts when they are far enough from the hole that they have difficulty even fantasizing about holing out.

large   Term of admiration for a well-hit drive. For example, "That is *large*! Anything flying that far should have a stewardess on it."

launched   Term for a drive that takes off like a Tomahawk cruise missile. A *launched* ball is usually *large* and vice versa.

lay the sod over it   Another term for hitting the ground behind the ball first. Theoretically, if you hit the ground firmly and far enough behind the ball, you may produce a divot that covers the undisturbed ball. (See also *fat, hit it*.)

lay up To aim short of the green and chip on rather than attempt a long or otherwise risky approach shot.

leaf rule Rule used in certain parts of America during autumn allowing a golfer to play another ball without penalty when his previous shot is lost and assumed covered by *leaves*. The *leaf rule* can cause a lot of arguments. You can protect against opponents invoking this rule by carrying a book of matches and gasoline in your golf bag.

leak oil What a golfer does as his game begins to fall apart. For *duffers* this process often begins at the first tee. With reference to the pros, this term is usually applied to a golfer who is leading a tournament but has begun to give away shots as his game disintegrates. Greg Norman has leaked more oil than the *Exxon Valdez*.

leaner A shot that comes to rest so close to the hole it appears to be *leaning* against the flagstick. A term usually associated with horseshoes or quoits.

lip The edge of the hole.

lip out A putt that hits the *lip* and spins out.

Liz Taylor A shot that's a little *fat* but still okay. Not to be confused with a *Roseanne,* which is very fat and not okay.

lockjaw Condition afflicting golfers who refuse to concede putts, even very short ones.

long and wrong Description of a golfer who can hit the ball long distances but seldom in the right direction. As the late, great Harvey Penick said, "The woods are full of long hitters."

looper Caddie.

lot of game Phrase describing a golfer who is excellent in all phases of the game. You say, "He certainly has a *lot of game*." Then you say, "I hate him."

lurking In stroke-play tournaments, a term used to describe a player who is poised to make a move toward the top of the leader board. In amateur golf, it describes the lecherous souls who frequent the *nineteenth hole*.

make the turn   When you move from the front side of the course to the back nine (tenth hole), you have *made the turn*. You probably also tallied your score for the first nine, which may *turn* your stomach.

meat and potatoes par four   A long, straightforward par four devoid of water, bunkers, and other hazards that might make the hole more difficult.

member's bounce   A lucky bounce that creates the illusion that a golfer is familiar with the course and knows how to play his shots accordingly.

Mickey Mouse course   A golf course with many flaws, possibly including poor maintenance, too many short holes, and tacky architectural features.

military golf "Left, right. Left, right." (See also *army golf.*)

milk the grip To lighten and tighten the grip on a club alternately before beginning a swing. This enables a golfer to get exactly the correct grip pressure (light) for a solid stroke.

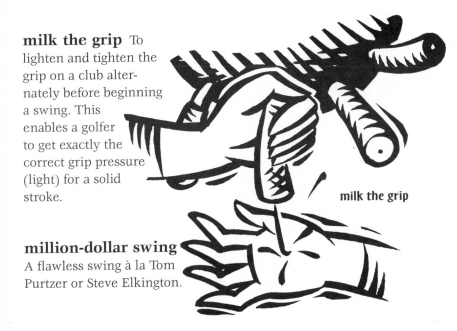

milk the grip

million-dollar swing A flawless swing à la Tom Purtzer or Steve Elkington.

Monday's children Marginal pros who competed on *Monday* mornings in an attempt to earn entry into that week's tournament in the dark days before the "all-exempt" PGA Tour.

money player The golfer who seems to make every big putt and come up with a good shot in every pressure situation.

move The golf swing. If you like what you see, you say, "He puts a good *move* on it."

moving day Saturday—the day in four-day professional tournaments when contenders attempt to move into position to win.

muff To mishit a shot.

mulligan A "takeover shot," used when a player *muffs* his first attempt. No score is official for any round in which you take a *mulligan*—a concept most of America's golfers seem to have a hard time understanding.

Nassau Probably the most popular form of golfing wager. It's a three-part bet with the front nine, the back nine, and the total match each being equally weighted wagers. The name comes from *Nassau* Country Club in New York, where the bet is said to have originated.

nasty A *nasty* is a *junk* bet you can cash in on if you hole a shot from off the putting surface and your score for that hole equals par or better.

natural, a A birdie made without the aid of any handicap strokes. Naturally, a *natural* always seems to happen on the tough holes, where handicap strokes are given. Easier holes, where no handicap strokes are available, often produce *natural* triple bogies.

neck, the Another way of saying *hosel*, or the socket in the head of a club where the shaft is inserted.

needle When you are verbally teasing and taunting your opponents, you are *needling* them or sticking in the *needle*. A good *needler* can really get under the skin of his competition.

never up, never in Admonition used after a putt is left short. In other words, another way to state the obvious.

nineteenth hole, the The bar and grill you visit after your round. This is the place where most golfers find their best lies.

nip it When you hit an iron shot without taking a divot, you have *nipped* it. Good golfers do this in an attempt to minimize backspin; bad golfers do it by accident.

nuked When you hit a shot that achieves the absolute
maximum distance for that club, you have *nuked* it. During
the 1991 PGA Championship at Crooked Stick, eventual champion and big hitter John Daly was *nuking* his sand wedge to
the tune of 148 yards. That's *big*!

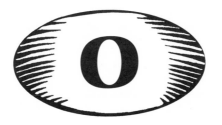

OB The abbreviation for the three saddest words in golf—*out of bounds*. You don't want to go there.

on fire You're *on fire* when everything you do on the course seems to work out just as you planned.

on the clock Condition under which a group of slow-playing professionals is informed by tournament officials that their play will be timed to ensure it is in accordance with the rules and continued slow play will result in a penalty—a warning that usually draws a response of incredulity and disdain from the golfers. This slow play by the guys on TV is largely responsible for the five- and six-hour rounds that are so common on public golf courses today.

on the screws Description for a well-executed shot. In the good ol' days, when woods were made of wood, club makers fitted a plastic insert into the club face as a safeguard against premature wear. These inserts were fastened to the club with *screws*. When a golfer would hit a good shot, he would say, "I hit it *on the screws*."

one a side When your *sandbagging* opponent insists that his handicap is two strokes higher than yours, you'll have to give him two strokes to make your match even. So you give him a stroke on the most difficult hole on each nine—*one a side*. Then you sit back and watch as he shoots sixty-eight.

open the door To misplay a shot that allows your opponent back into a hole, a match, or the tournament.

Oscar Brown Nickname used by some of the funnier golfers for out of bounds, but only when their opponent hits it *OB*. As in "Sorry, pal, that's *Oscar Brown*." Time to *reload*.

overcook it To hit a shot too hard. Also, when you intentionally draw, fade, slice, or hook a shot and you get too much curvature, you've *overcooked it*.

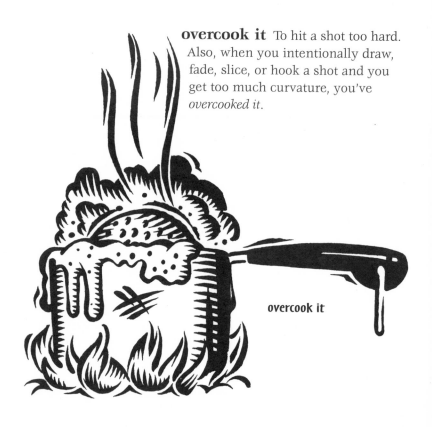

overcook it

paint job A pro's putt that *lips out*. The holes in professional tournaments are painted white to make it easier for TV viewers to see their location, and sometimes the paint around the hole's edge becomes crusty and makes the lip less accommodating to putts. At least that's what the pros say.

peg Tee.

pencil bag A small, thin golf bag often used by kids to lighten the load. Also called a *summer bag* because it's used in hot weather.

pencil hockey When someone (not you, of course) is charged with the awesome responsibility of keeping score and then cheats by recording erroneous scores, he is said to be playing *pencil hockey*, which is akin to horse thievery and subject to the same punishment—hanging!

pick it To hit the ball and make little or no contact with the ground. Accomplished with a sweeping motion as opposed to the sharp angle with which a *digger* attacks the ball. A golfer who picks the ball is called a *picker*. Greg Norman is a *picker*.

pick it up A term used to concede a putt. After your opponent has boxed the ball around four or five times, you can graciously suggest that he *pick it up*.

pigeon An easy mark—the golfer everybody wants to play against. If you hear anyone refer to you as a *pigeon*, take up chess.

pill The ball. The object of your frustration. Maybe instead of trying to hit the *pill*, you should take a *pill*.

pill

pin high Whenever the ball lies at the same elevation as the hole.

pinch A short, crisp shot played with firm wrists, no divot, and little follow-through.

pin-seeker A shot that heads right for the flagstick from the moment it leaves the club face.

pipeline The center of the fairway, so named because an irrigation pipe often runs down it.

pitch and putt A derisive term given to golf courses that are short and easily conquered, so named because just a pitch and a putt will get you into the hole.

plate A yardage marker that many courses have embedded into their fairways. A red *plate* means you are 100 yards from the center of the green, white is 150 yards, and blue is 200. If you're more than 200 yards from the green, don't bother looking for a *plate*. What you need is a miracle.

plateaued Term that refers to greens that are flat and sit up significantly higher than the level of the fairway.

play 'em down To play the ball as it lies. The only way to fly.

plugged When your ball becomes imbedded in the ground, it is *plugged*.

point A betting unit on a hole.

pond ball A golf ball specifically intended for shots over water. Usually *pond balls* are old, beat-up balls that don't constitute much of a loss if they find the water, which is exactly where they normally end up.

pop A short, crisp, abbreviated stroke on a putt.

pose What a golfer does when he hits a shot he's especially proud of, holding his follow-through for everyone to admire.

position A The ideal position from which to attack the pin.

preferred lie A euphemistic way of saying a golfer has improved his lie. This can be done legally in certain situations, but mostly it's done to cheat.

press A betting term that means a new match is starting within the original match. This *press* match continues until the end of the original match, and the stakes are the same for both matches. *Presses* are often automatic when one side goes down two holes in the original match.

pro side The high side of the hole, so called because more aggressive players generally miss their putts on the high side, where the ball has a greater chance of falling into the cup.

pro tees The tees from which the golf course plays the longest. The tees you do not want to play.

pull To hit the ball straight to the left of the intended target. *Pulled* shots do not curve, they head for trouble on a straight line.

punch Identical to a *knockdown* shot. A low, boring shot played with little wrist action and little follow-through. Used to combat a headwind.

pure it To strike the ball perfectly and achieve the intended ball flight and distance.

push The opposite of *pull*. To hit a shot that flies straight to the right of the intended target. A *push* does not curve, it heads straight for trouble without any side spin. Greg Norman *pushes* when the pressure's on.

put a tack on it A request from one of your fellow competitors to mark your ball, usually just before he holes a twenty-five-footer that breaks your heart.

putt out When you elect to finish a hole, even though you may not be away, you are *putting out*. It's permissible to do this if you declare your intentions before doing so and are just a few feet from the hole.

quacker See *duck hook*.

quail high A mishit shot flying *very* low to the ground.

quick When you rush your swing, your putting stroke, or your overall playing routine, you are getting *quick*. This usually results in poor play.

rainmaker A
shot that is hit
very high,
so called
because it
travels close
to the clouds.

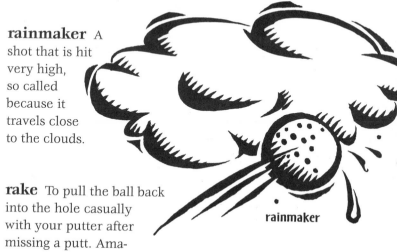

rainmaker

rake To pull the ball back
into the hole casually
with your putter after
missing a putt. Ama-
teurs often miss these *rake jobs* and then still count the stroke as
holed because they only made a token effort. That's cheating.

rattle it in When a putt bounces around the hole a bit before
dropping into the cup, a golfer has *rattled it in*. This usually
occurs when a putt has been struck firmly into the hole.

ready golf   In *ready golf* each player may "fire when ready," a procedure instituted to speed up play.

Red Grange   A score of seventy-seven, named after the number worn by the football great.

reload   To hit an errant tee shot and tee up a second ball. A term also used each time the beer cart approaches, as in "Let's *reload*."

ringer   A good player who enters a competition under less than truthful circumstances, usually by claiming a handicap that is much higher than it should be. Also known as a *sandbagger.*

rinse, a   What you give your ball when you clean it in a ball washer—or in the lake.

robbed Golfers love to complain about being *robbed*, usually when a putt doesn't break when it should have, or when a putt traveling at Mach 2 doesn't fall into the hole as it should have, or when a tee shot forty yards off line winds up six inches out of bounds. If you want to be cool on the golf course, don't whine about being *robbed* every time something doesn't go your way.

rock, the The *pill*. The ball.

roll it When somebody's a good putter, you say, "Man, he can really *roll it*." *Roll* can also be used when players *roll the ball over* in the fairway to get an improved lie.

roller coaster An up-and-down round.

rope hook Term for a low, hard hook that will run great distances after hitting the ground. Very bad.

routine Term used facetiously to describe a par that is made under anything but routine circumstances. For example, if you hole out an eighty-yard wedge shot for par, you might exclaim, "Another *routine* par, my friend."

run Whenever the ball is moving along the ground, it is said to be *running*. This is also what you should do if you bet and then don't have enough money to cover your losses.

S-word Ssssssh! This is a very bad word in golf. A s*hank* is a shot that flies ninety degrees to the right after the ball has been struck with the club's hosel. So devastating is this affliction that if you get the *shanks,* the best thing to do is leave the course immediately and seek professional help—from your bartender.

sandbagger A golfer who falsely posts high scores in order to inflate his handicap, thereby making him more difficult to defeat in matches. This is *serious* cheating. Also known as a *ringer*.

sandy When you escape from a bunker to make birdie or par, you've made a *sandy*. One of many *junk* bets golfers make during a match.

scats A betting game in which all the members of a group play against each other for a predetermined amount on each hole. Ties carry over to the next hole.

scrambler A golfer who plays somewhat erratically but manages to salvage good scores from inconsistent play. A *scramble* refers to a golf competition in which each of four players on a team hits a tee shot and picks a best ball, then plays a second shot from that spot. The team continues to pick a best ball and play from that spot until a shot is holed.

scrape it around To play spotty or inconsistent golf but still manage to post a good score. Great pros like Jack Nicklaus stay in tournament contention by *scraping it around* on days when they don't have their *A game.*

scratch Term to describe a golfer who has a zero handicap; that is, he is starting from *scratch.* Dream on.

scuff A lousy shot that results from hitting the ground before hitting the ball. (See also *fat, hit it.*)

set them up What you do when you improve your lie in the fairway. Also what you ask the bartender to do after you've taken money from your archrival. (See also *roll it*.)

shag bag Any container used by a golfer to hold practice balls.

shape it To curve a shot intentionally to fit the hole. Corey Pavin is the absolute best at this.

shooting the lights out Hitting all the shots and making low scores.

short grass Where you are when you hit the fairway with your drive.

short hole Term used to describe any par three.

short stick The putter, so named because it's the *shortest* club in the bag. You can make up for a lot of bad work with other sticks if you can handle the *short stick*.

shotgun start Some tournaments station players on each tee to start a round so that they can all finish at roughly the same time. This is called a *shotgun start* because the beginning of play was once signaled by a *shotgun* blast. Now they use a horn to signal the beginning of play—it's a lot safer.

side Each nine holes—front and back. Also each team in a competition.

sitter

sitter Term for a ball *sitting* atop the grass in the rough. Pray for a *sitter* when you see your tee shot heading for trouble.

skull To hit the top half of the ball with the bottom edge of an iron. This shot comes out low and fast and usually *runs* much farther than desired.

sky To pop the ball straight up into the air. You won't be happy with the distance of the shot.

slam-dunk To hit the ball into the hole with great force. This usually happens when a putt or chip that is moving much faster than the ideal speed slams into the back of the cup, pops into the air, and falls into the hole.

slice A shot that curves to the right. The most common fault of amateur golfers, generally caused by an open club face at impact.

slick Term used to describe fast greens.

slider A putt that breaks slightly and subtly in either direction. Also a low, hard left-to-right shot. Fred Couples hits lots of *sliders* off the tee.

smile Balls that are *skulled* or otherwise mishit often wind up with a cut on their surface that resembles a *smile*, though you won't be smiling as you reach into your bag for another ball.

smoked Term for a ball that is hit hard and far.

smother hook A *hook* that flies left and low to the ground, though only for a short distance; it is struck with a severely closed club face.

snake A long putt that breaks in more than one direction. One of the most famous *snakes* ever holed was a sixty-footer by Ben Crenshaw on the tenth hole at Augusta National Golf Club during the 1984 Masters Tournament.

snap hook See *duck hook* and *rope hook*.

sniper See *duck hook, rope hook,* and *snap hook*, all names for the same crummy shot.

snowman A score of eight for a hole, so named because the digit resembles a *snowman*. Also called lots of unprintable names. (See also *Frosty*.)

spinach The roughest of the rough. When you were a kid, you hated *spinach* for the taste. Now, as a mature, open-minded adult golfer, you hate *spinach* because you can't play a decent shot out of the stuff. (See also *cabbage*.)

spinach

spraying Term that means your shot pattern is all over the place and your misses are about as predictable as the weather.

stake it To knock the ball really close to the hole (*stake*). (See also *leaner*.)

stand on it What you do when you swing your hardest, to get maximum distance out of a club.

stick Short for flag*stick*. Also, a shot that hits and stops quickly is said to *stick* to the green.

sticks Your clubs. When your tee shot lands near the hole, your competitor might ask, "What *stick* did you use?" Then you hold up five fingers to identify the three iron you just hit.

stiff Term used to describe a ball hit very close to the hole. Also, when a club shaft has very little bend, it is a *stiff* shaft. And when you don't tip your caddie after the round, you *stiff* him.

stoney When a golfer knocks the ball to within *gimme* range, it is *stone* dead, or *stoney*.

stop the bleeding Finally to make a par or birdie after several less than stellar holes.

striped it To hit a good tee shot.

suck back A ball that hits the green and then reverses direction due to backspin is said to have *sucked back*. As far as amateur golfers are concerned, this phrase is useful only as a spectator, since amateurs rarely generate enough backspin to get a ball to *suck back*.

sucker pin A pin that is cut so close to a hazard that only a *sucker* would fire right at it.

swing doctor A teaching professional. Consult with caution; often the cure is worse than the disease.

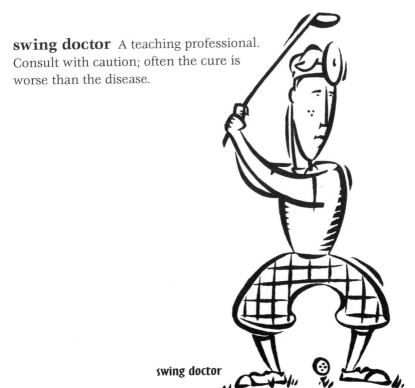

swing doctor

take it deep To shoot a *very* low score. (See also *shooting the lights out*.)

talk to it Golfers are always issuing pleas or instructions to their ball. "Get up!" "Get down!" "Sit." "Bite." It's fun, and there's no rule against it, so go ahead and *talk to it*.

tap in A short, easy putt that anyone can make. (See also *gimme*.)

tester A putt that's long enough so that it's not a *gimme* but short enough so that a decent player should hole it, so called because it *tests* a golfer's skill.

Texas wedge When you use your putter from off the green, that club becomes a *Texas wedge*, so named because the shot became popular in Texas, where hard, dry conditions make it less risky to putt from off the green.

that dog will hunt Expression golfers use after they've hit a good shot. It is derived from *hunting*, where certain *dogs* are better *hunters* than others. So it is with golf shots.

that dog will hunt

that's good When you want to let an opponent know that you are conceding a putt you say, "*That's good.*"

thin, hit it To hit the ball in the center with the club's leading edge, instead of sliding under it. Chances are your shot will fly lower and farther than you intended. This is still much better than *hitting it fat*.

three-jack Three putts on a single green. Very bad, indeed.

throw-up range Any putt that's short enough so a good player should make it, but long enough so that he's nervous about missing it, is in *throw-up range*. Players don't really throw up over these putts, they just miss them. (See also *yips* and *knee-knocker*.)

tight If there is very little cushion (grass) between the ball and God's earth, you have a *tight* lie. If the guys in your group don't want to play for some cash, they're *tight*.

tips, the The tees from which the course plays the longest.

toe The part of the club head farthest from the club shaft. If you hit a ball out there you *toed* it, or hit a *toe job*, and it will probably travel on a right-to-left flight path.

top To strike the top part of the ball with the club's bottom edge. A *topped shot* will only roll a short distance along the ground.

tossing balls An easy way to decide who will be partners during a competitive match between four players. One golfer takes a ball from each player and then *tosses* them all into the air simultaneously. Whoever owns the two balls coming to rest closest to each other are partners, as are the two remaining players. This expression is not to be confused with the dastardly act of freeing oneself from a bunker using the *hand mashie.* That act is known as *cheating.*

touch   A player with an aptitude for playing short, delicate shots around the green has a deft *touch*. He is a *touch* player. *Touch* shots don't require strength, but call for a certain feel for how the ball will react when struck and when it lands on the green. Seve Ballesteros is one example of a great *touch* player. Unfortunately for Seve, he can no longer hit the planet with a tee shot, so his great *touch* does him little good.

track   The golf course. When *track* is preceded by *dog*, it's time to look for a new place to play.

tracking Term that refers to a putt hit on a perfect line to the hole. Putts that are *tracking* don't always go into the hole, as sometimes the speed is wrong, but they are *tracking* toward the center of the cup when they run out of speed.

trap A geek's term for bunker. There are no such things as *traps*, only bunkers.

trouble shot Whenever you hit a shot into a place where you don't have an easy path to the green, you are in *trouble*, so your next shot will be a *trouble shot.* For *hackers* this constitutes every shot not played from the tee or the green.

trouble wood Any wood with a loft greater than that of a five wood. The most popular is the seven wood, a club used effectively from deep rough and fairway bunkers. These clubs are especially popular with seniors and women, two groups who need help hitting the ball higher. They have much more success hitting *trouble woods* than long irons.

turn it over To move the ball from right to left, that is, to hit a draw. Never say this if you want the ball to move from left to right. If you want to move the ball in that direction, just say, "I want to *cut* it."

ugly Anything bad that happens to you on the course, especially when you hit a poor shot, is *ugly*. So when you hit an incredibly bad shot, don't curse, just say, "Man, that was *ugly*," and everyone will nod with understanding.

up and down A way of describing the short game; if you chip on and then one-putt, you're *up and down* in two. Also, when your level of play alternates between good and bad, you're having an *up-and-down* round.

upshoot A shot hit with a higher-than-anticipated trajectory to a point short of the target. Also called *ballooning*.

U-turn A putt that rolls all the way around the edge of the cup before coming out.

valleys On an undulating green, the relatively flat areas between mounds. The most famous *valley* is the *Valley* of Sin, located on the eighteenth green at the Old Course, St. Andrews, Scotland.

victory lap The circle a putt makes around the rim of the cup before falling in.

victory lap

waggle To move the club head back and forth before beginning the takeaway. Golfers do this to relieve tension just before beginning their swing. When they see the results of their swing, tension reenters their bodies.

wagon A stupid name for a stupid contraption—the golf cart.

watery grave Where your disobedient balls go every time you try to carry a water hazard.

weekend warriors Golfers who play infrequently, so called because the only time they can play is on *weekends*.

whiff When you swing at the ball and miss.

whoa down A golfer's plea for his putt to stop rolling.

wind cheater A low, driving shot that is effective into a headwind. Amateurs often use this term after they've unintentionally hit a low, straight shot.

windmill hole A poorly designed hole named after the finishing hole on some miniature golf courses.

winter rules In certain areas where the *winters* are harsh, golf courses don't receive much maintenance between October and April. To make *winter* golf more palatable in these areas, many courses enact *winter rules*, which provide for improved lies under certain circumstances. *Winter rules* are fair since golf was not meant to be played on a poorly maintained course, though the Scots play on rough courses year-round.

wolf A betting game for three or four players that allows one player on each hole (the honor rotates among the players) to go it alone against the others in the group, thereby getting a chance to win three bets on one hole. This player also has the option of choosing a partner for the hole. The player who decides to go it alone is the *wolf*, a lone *wolf*.

woodpecker An errant shot into the woods that bounces off a few trees—and makes a noise similar to the bird of the same name.

work the ball To hit the ball high, low, right to left, or left to right on demand. Corey Pavin can *work the ball* any way he wants. Jack Nicklaus prefers to *work the ball* left to right and has made a damn good living doing just that.

worm burner A low shot that buzzes along just inches from the ground—and the *worms*.

worm burner

X What you put on your scorecard when you do not finish a hole. A common optical illusion makes it look like a four or a five.

yank A putt that is *pulled* to the left.

yips A nervous disorder that afflicts golfers on the green. An inability to take the putter back, coupled with twitchy hands and the complete absence of nerve, constitutes a case of the *yips*. No golfer has ever permanently conquered this condition.

you da man! A popular expression among golf's great unwashed, generally heard in the millisecond after a shot has been struck and well before the outcome of the shot can be determined. This is very annoying to *da man* when his shot lands in a lake.

zone, the When everything you do is right, and you know it's right before you do it, that's *the zone*. The number of times you get to visit *the zone*, and the amount of time you spend there, is in direct proportion to your ability. So if you want to get in *the zone,* you'd better visit the practice tee first.